CON CHO
PRE-SCHOOL

LESSON PLAN

GRADE: _______________

SUBJECT: _______________

PREPARED BY: _______________

MON

TUES

WED

THURS

FRI

MATERIALS

• KHI • CHO •

Counting Dogs and Monkeys

AN ADDITION GAME

Directions: Count how many of each animal you see. Write the answers in the box provided below.

Monkeys

Dogs

NAME THAT SHAPE!

Can you name these shapes?

Name ______________________ Date ______________________

Class ______________________ Score ______________________

FUN WITH CHO!

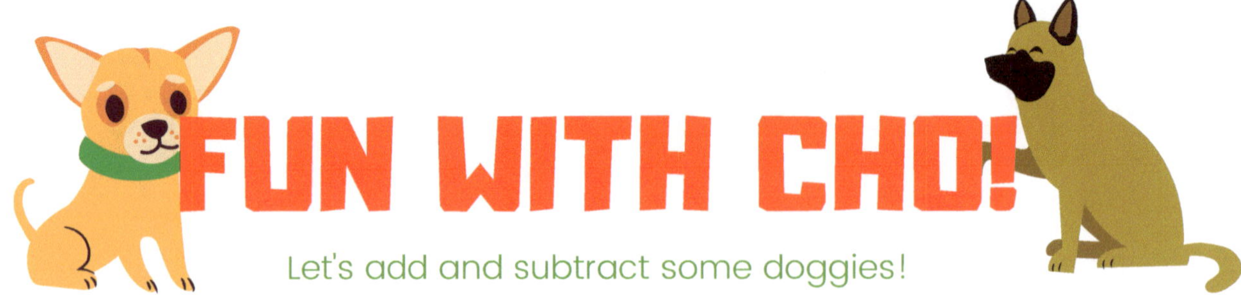

Let's add and subtract some doggies!

Add or subtract the dogs.
Write the correct answer on the space provided.

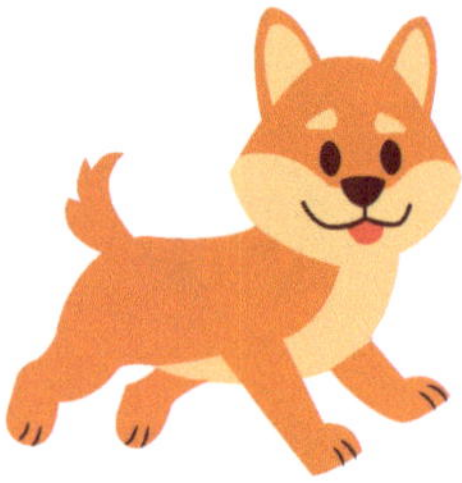 + 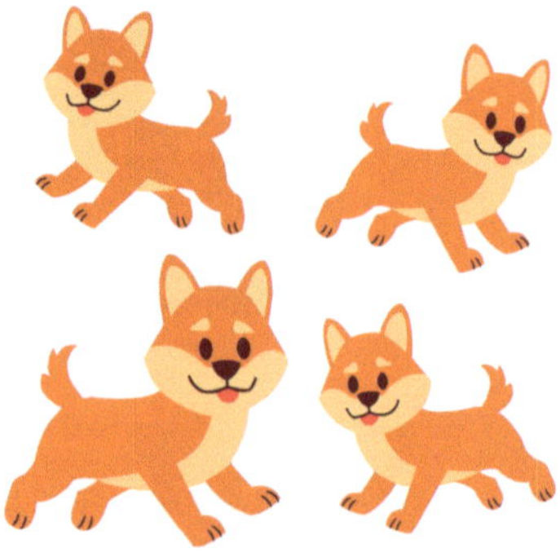 =

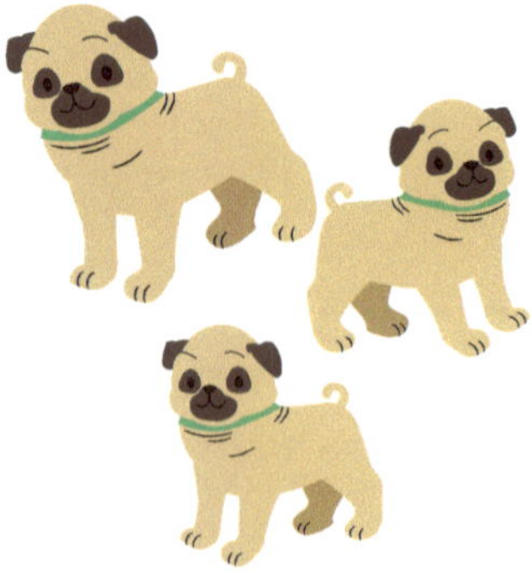 − 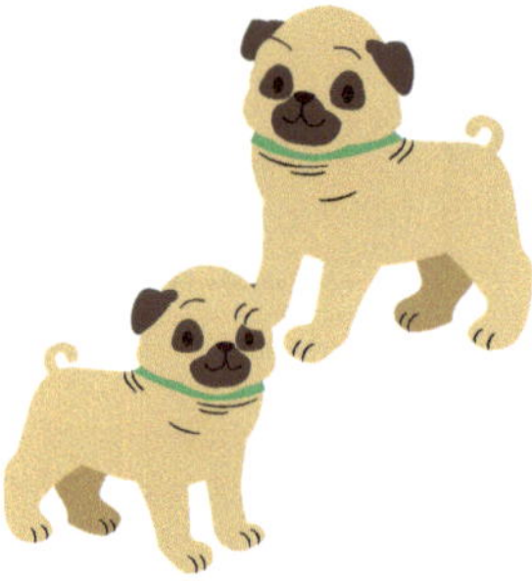 =

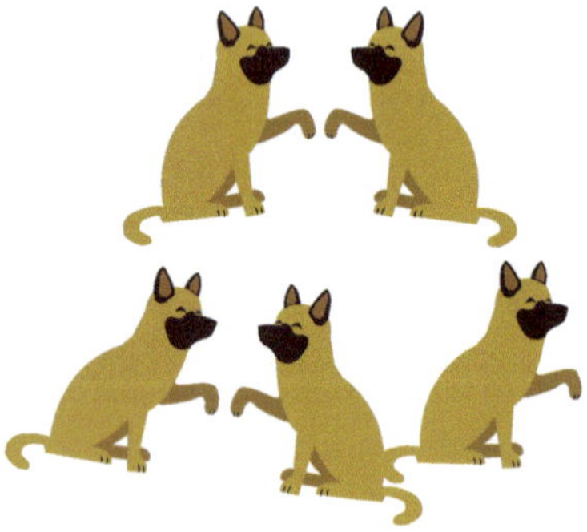 − 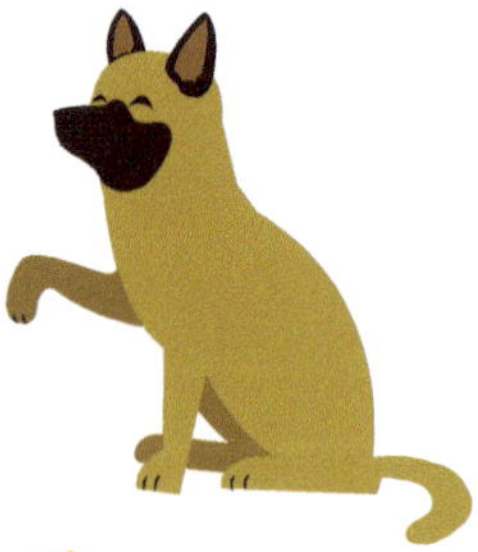 =

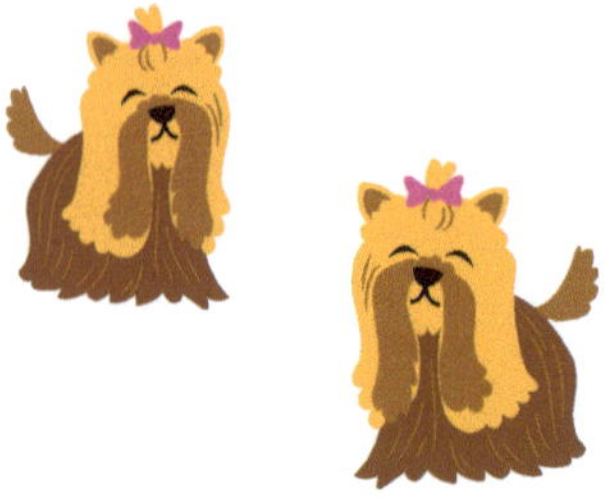 + 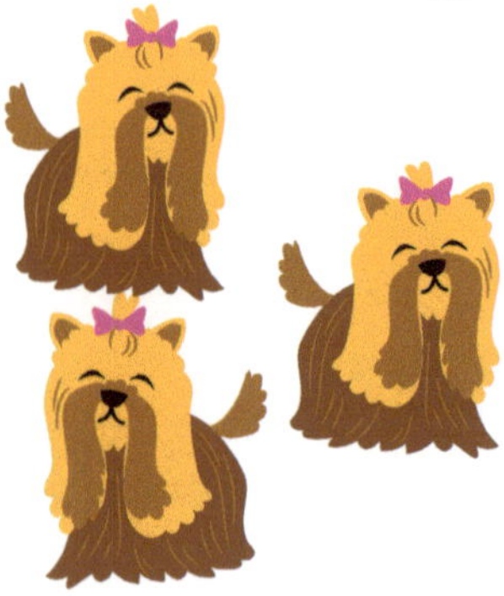 =

LET'S COLOR LETTERS

Color the uppercase letters <u>red.</u>
Color the lowercase letters <u>blue</u>.

• KHI • CHO •

MONKEY MATH

Solve the equations to feed the Monkeys!

Name ___________________ Date ___________________

Class ___________________ Score ___________________

THE MISSING LETTER

Look at the pictures below. Say what you see out loud. What do you hear?
Add the missing letter on the blank.

_ a t

b _ x

m a _

_ u g

p _ n

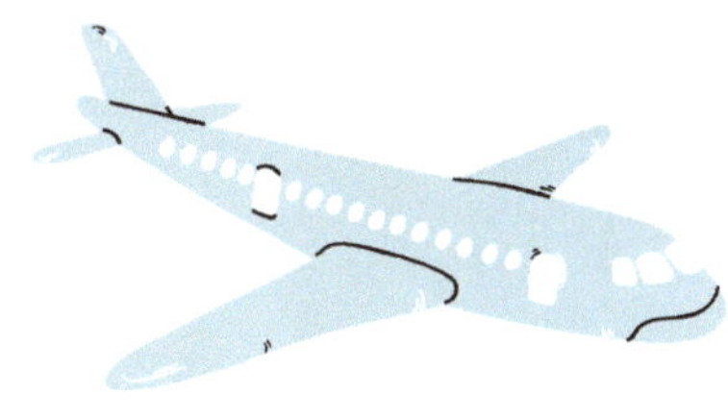

j e _

_ e g

v _ n

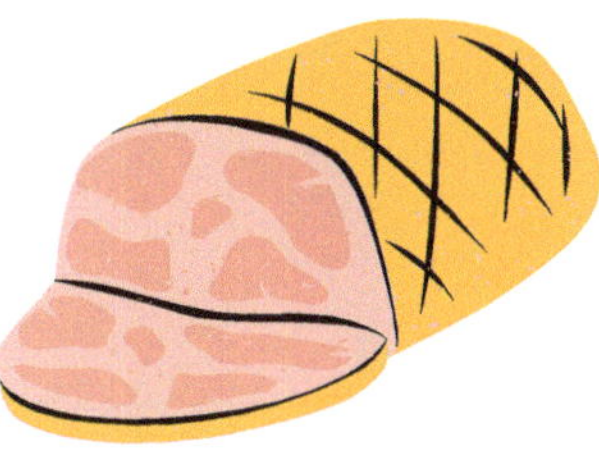

h a _

Identifying Objects

Read the sentences and color the correct object.

I see a cookie 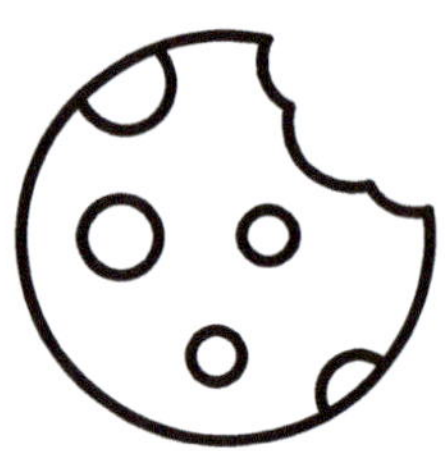  

I see a book   

I see a bird 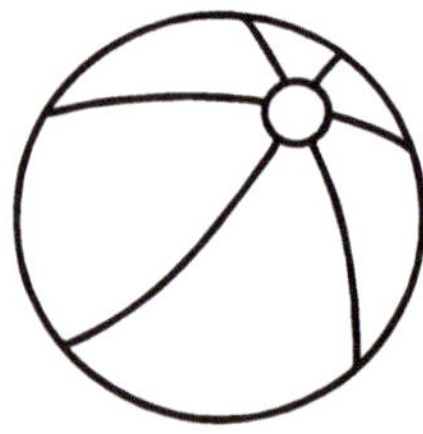  

I see a candle   

I see a nest   

BARREL FULL OF MONKEYS

Figure out how many monkeys are in the barrel!

There are several monkeys going to this barrel party! Count
how many monkeys there are in total!

COUNT THE SPOTS!

Count the brown and white spots on this dog! Write how many each of them are, then write the total number on the blank.

Brown _______   White _________   Total: _______

Letter Sounds

Say the name of each picture out loud and circle the beginning sound.

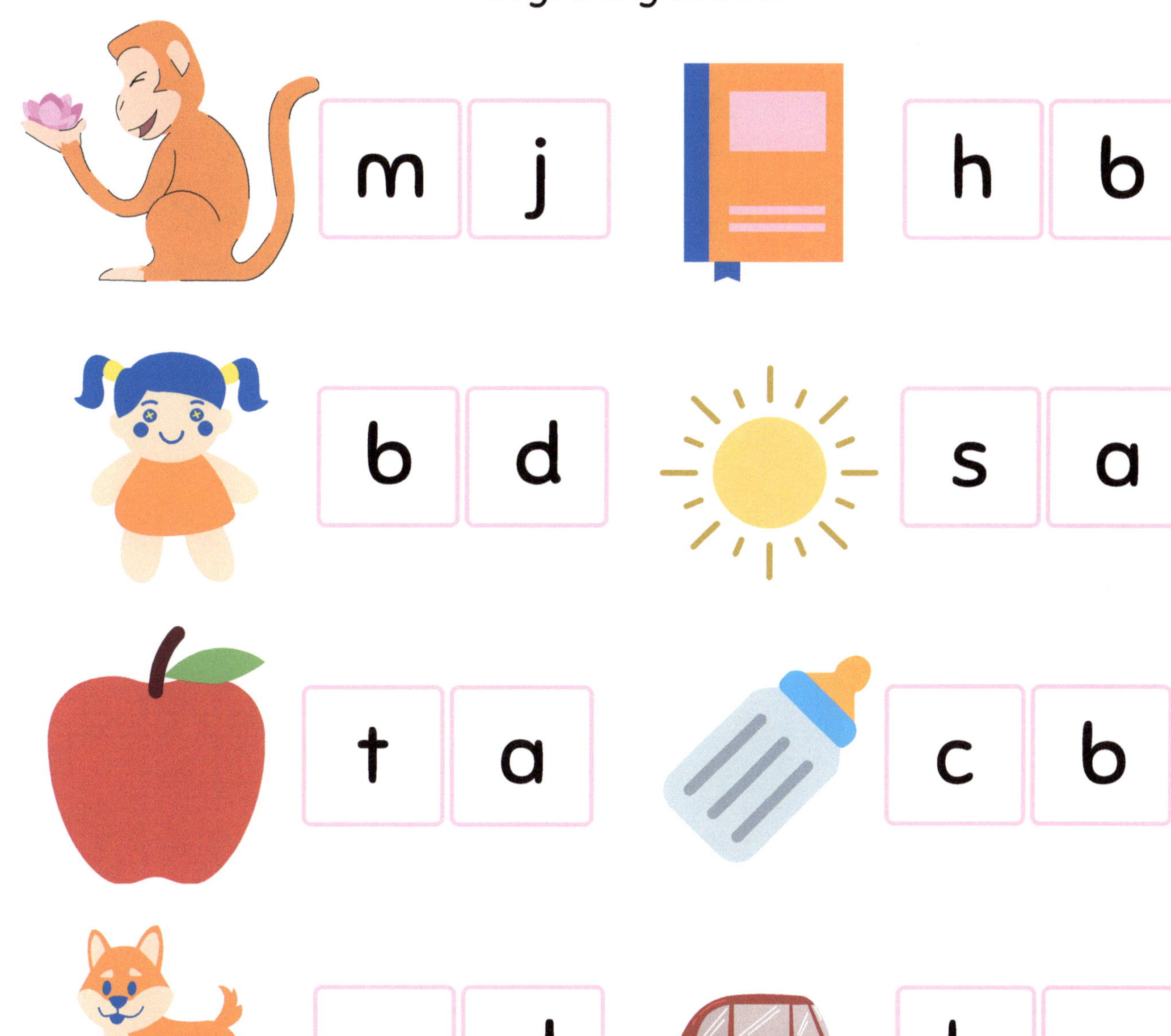

Notes

Notes

Notes

Notes

Notes

Notes

Notes

Notes

Notes

Notes

Notes

Notes

Notes

Notes

Notes

Notes